Dear readers,

A couple months ago as I tucked my daughter into bed she nonchalantly asked me, "Mom, am I autistic?" It caught me off guard because in our house the word autism is heard quite often, but we don't label anyone. When my friends come over with their autistic children we don't point it out, we just treat everyone with kindness and respect; label not needed. I simply said, "Yes, you are, you have a type of autism called Asperger's Syndrome. You were diagnosed with Asperger's Syndrome and hypotonia when you were two." To which she said, "Oh, is that why you work so hard on the magazine and write books about autism?" "YES! Yes, it is but not just for you but to help other parents because it took mommy a long time to get you help so I try to share what I have learned to help other parents," I tried to explain. Then she said, "Is my brother autistic too? Is it why he has a hard time speaking?" My eyes started to tear at her realization and I said, "Yes, my love, your brother is autistic, too." She said, "Does he have the same kind as me?" Again I was speechless for a good while. I thought about all the autistic adults that I hold in such high regard, that have taught me so much including the importance about not assigning functioning labels and how many have felt very strongly when the makers of the DSM-V changed everything. So I tried to explain to her that they stop diagnosing people with Asperger's and PDD-NOS and all the others and now everyone is just diagnosed as having Autistic Spectrum Disorder. She turned to me and simply said, "Well, that was a dumb idea." To which I burst out laughing.

This month's issue is all about the important talks that you have to have with your children. Our cover story is done by the talented Cynthia Kim and explains several aspects of speaking to your child about more than just genitalia when it comes to puberty. Thankfully, our Life Coach Jaclyn Hunt was kind enough to answer all the scientific puberty questions and how to handle both the girl and boy talks about body changes. In addition to that we are excited to welcome M.Kelter to our team of writers who wrote about what he wishes he knew about friendship in hopes that we can help lay the groundwork for our children. Plus Kimberlee McCafferty "autism talk

Bill Wong, the only certified autistic OT, join our team here at Autism Parenting and can't wait to share all of his great advice.

I would like to thank all of you that have had kind words and have shown your support during this past month. My first children's book has been released Grace Figures Out School which is a book meant for all children to start the conversation about autism and treating everyone equally and respectfully. It touches on common struggles like sensory issues, and difficulty understanding figurative language. You can check it out here https://www.tatepublishing.com/bookstore/book.php?w=978-1-62902-855-2.

Also, the release of my second reference book, Early Signs of Autism, has been released at the beginning of this month in an effort to help parents decide whether or not to seek a diagnosis. It is a combination of my story and several months of research. Often parents find too much information leaving them overwhelmed and they don't have the time to read a lengthy book, which is why I tried to provide an informative guide in under 60 pages. http://www.amazon.com/Early-Autism-Toddlers-Infants-Babies/dp/1495297071

Kind Regards,
Leslie A. Burby
Editor-in-Chief

Disclaimer:
Autism Parenting Magazine tries our best to deliver honest, unbiased reviews, resources, and advice but please note that due to the variety of capabilities of people on the spectrum that these are recommendations and are not guaranteed by Autism Parenting Magazine or its writers.

Table of contents

7 If you could talk to your teen self
Body changes isn't the only thing that needs to be discussed
Author: M. Kelter

12 Benefits of Pinterest for Professionals and Parents
Using Pinterest to help get the latest OT (occupational therapy) ideas
Author: Bill Wong OTD, OTR/L

14 Engaging the Community of a Child with Autism
Getting everyone to use their strengths to help your child have fun learning new skills
Author: Michael Cameron

17 AUTISM IN THE NEWS: A NEW YEAR AND NEW HOPE
Hope that in the future autistics will be treated respectfully if not by AS at least by others
Author: Megan Kelly

20 THE AUTISM TALK
Answering your child when they ask if they have autism
Author: Kim McCafferty

22 BOOK IN THE SPOTLIGHT: AUTISM AND THE WORLD ACCORDING TO MATT
A memoir chronicling her son's journey into living independently
Author: Liz Becker

4 Q&A SECTION: DISCUSSING PUBERTY WITH YOUR CHILD
Our Life Coach answers the tough questions about explaining puberty and body changes with great additional resources
Author: Jaclyn Hunt

28 BINS AND PENCIL HELP
Sensory fun activities to do at home with your child and solutions for pencil grip
Author: Leslie Burby

29 YOUR DAY, YOUR WAY
The Autism/Special Needs Daily Organizer App
Author: Brooke Twine

31 HOW I WISH I KNEW MY FATHER HAD ASPERGER'S SYNDROME
The insight of one woman's feelings about her lack of a father-daughter relationship and suggestions to foster better relationships for Aspergian fathers
Author: Dr. Mary Houser

Disclaimer: Please note that the advertised business and products are not endorsed or guaranteed by Autism Parenting Magazine or any of it's employees.

DAUGHTER'S PERSPECTIVE

Beyond the Talk: What Else Autistic Tweens and Teens Need to Know About Puberty

by Cynthia Kim

> When it came to puberty, my parents did what many parents in the seventies did: they gave me a book about puberty written especially for girls. It was a slim cranberry hardback with an ambiguous title like **Everything is Changing**.

I was a voracious reader, so I would curl up in my beanbag and scour the pages for clues to the mysterious changes that were on the horizon. I think I had many of the same fears, anxieties and curiosities about puberty as my friends. Certainly my body went through the same changes that other girls experienced. However, I think there are some areas where tweens and teens on the spectrum would benefit from additional information or guidance.

In addition to talking to your autistic son or daughter about all of the things parents normally cover when talking about puberty, consider discussing the following when you feel the timing and circumstances are right:

1. HYGIENE

- Talk about where body odor comes from and why. Be sure to mention that sometimes we can't detect our own body odor but others can.
- Emphasize the importance of regular showers, tooth brushing, mouthwash, deodorant, and changes of clothing in preventing body odor. Not everyone will need to shower every day and some autistic youngsters may have sensory sensitivities that make showering unpleasant. Washing the face, underarms and genitals with a washcloth can help reduce unwanted odors between showers.

You may have to repeat hygiene instructions or reminders many times. You may need to come up with a visual or text schedule to hang in the bathroom. There are still days when I need a reminder to do basic self-care tasks. This isn't "one and done" instruction for many autistic individuals.

If you notice that the new stick of deodorant is lasting far too long or there aren't enough pairs of underwear showing up in the laundry to account for daily changes, a fact finding mission might be in order. Maybe the deodorant smells too strongly or feels sticky. Maybe two pairs of underwear are comfortable and the other ten aren't.

Rather than asking, "Why aren't you _____?," which can make kids feel defensive, try a softer approach like, "How did you like that deodorant we picked out? If it's too smelly, we can try a different kind." Maybe your child hates it and doesn't know how to tell you. This stuff can be embarrassing when it's so new and confusing.

DAUGHTER'S PERSPECTIVE

2. SOCIAL SKILLS

Typical children experience significant advances in social skills during the tween and teen years. This is a time when the gap in social skills can become painfully obvious or even dangerous for autistic youngsters. Use your judgment to decide on an age-appropriate time to introduce the following social skills concepts.

- Talk about appropriate and inappropriate ways that people express interest in each other. Give specific age-appropriate verbal and nonverbal examples.
- Talk about how to say no and what to do if someone doesn't take "no" seriously. Even if you've been talking about this with your child since they were small, now is a good time to reinforce it, with specific examples of situations in which saying no may be confusing or hard.
- Explain what flirting is and why people do it. Give age-appropriate examples of verbal and nonverbal flirting cues that teens might use.
- Explain the concept of personal space and boundaries, including how a person signals that they do or don't want another person to come closer or to touch them.
- Talk about types of touch, specifically the differences between how friends touch each other (on the arm, on the shoulder, quick platonic hugs) and how boyfriends/girlfriends touch each other (holding hands, on the face, longer hugs).
- Talk about media stereotypes and how real-life romantic relationships are different from those your child might be seeing on TV, in movies or in books.

If you're already working on social skills with your child, romantic partner interaction can be presented as a new social skill to be learned like any other. Be specific. Use lots of examples, perhaps drawing on movies, TV shows or some time spent people-watching at the mall food court. The wider variety of examples you provide the better. Remember, autism makes it hard to generalize from one situation to another.

Don't assume that autistic teens will extrapolate from middle school social skills to high school skills the way typical teens often do. Continue to update your child's knowledge bank as he or she gets older. How people express interest in each other is an appropriate topic for tweens and younger teens. An older teen needs specific knowledge about what a romantic advance looks like and how to verbally and nonverbally signal acceptance or rejection in an appropriate way. They also need to know when they are giving off "I'm interested" signals, especially if those signals might be unintentional.

This may not seem like rocket science to a typical adult. Most young men and women instinctively pick up the verbal and nonverbal language of flirting, but for someone who struggles with reading body language, it can be mind boggling. I'm 44, fairly intelligent, in a long-term relationship . . . and I still have only the vaguest idea of what flirting looks like in action.

3. SENSORY ISSUES

- Include your preteen or teen in choices of new hygiene products like deodorant, body spray, razors, shaving cream, pads or tampons. Sensitivity to smell can make perfumed items (including tampons) hard to tolerate.
- Tactile sensitivities may impact your child's choices and comfort level with clothing. Boys may chafe at having to wear a tie or dress pants made of synthetic material. Girls may find a newly introduced bra especially difficult. Don't be surprised if your child seems intent on clinging to more comfortable "childish" clothing, even as peers move on to trendier styles. Help him or her find age-appropriate clothing that's comfortable.
- Changing bodies can mean changing sensory sensitivities. Some teens might be sensitive to having body hair or facial hair; others might be sensitive to shaving. Also, changing body shape can make clothes feel "weird" or uncomfortable in places that they weren't before.
- Sensory sensitivities can make romantic interaction unpleasant. While the typical teen might be excited about a first kiss, a teen with tactile sensitivities might not enjoy kissing or romantic touching. Let your teen know that this is okay and that they don't have to pretend to like something for the sake of fitting in, even if it's something that everyone else seems to enjoy.
- For girls, be alert to the role hypo- or hypersensitivity to pain can play in menstruation. I used to get cramps so bad that my legs would feel numb and often that was the complaint I voiced. I'm sure my "numb legs" made little sense to the school nurse as a symptom of menstruation.

DAUGHTER'S PERSPECTIVE

Depending on your son or daughter's interests, personality and sensory sensitivities, they may be interested in hairstyles, clothing and other things popular with kids their age, or they may not. They might become interested in those things at a later age than their peers. They might want to try some of them out, but only if they can do so while not aggravating sensory sensitivities.

Honestly, there's no typical autistic teen when it comes to personal grooming preferences. You might have a daughter who can barely be bothered to run a brush through her hair or you might have a daughter with a special interest in eyeliner that threatens to break the bank. The same goes for boys--you might have a son who forgets to change his shirt for a week if you don't remind him or you have might have a guy who has a meltdown because he's unexpectedly run out of his favorite hair gel.

4. HORMONES!

I've saved this one for last because it's a bit scary. The hormonal changes of puberty and adolescence are hard on typical teens. For teens on the spectrum, they can seriously throw things out whack. Before puberty, I'd never had a full-on meltdown. Hormones turned me into a shouting, door-slamming, crying mess. And the worst part was, most of the time I had no idea why. It all felt completely irrational.

Be alert to hormonal changes in your son or daughter as they go through puberty. This may be a time when other conditions like anxiety or mood disorders arise. You may see an increase in stimming or other self-comforting behavior. It may be when your son's need for alone time skyrockets or you feel like your daughter is backsliding in social skills, emotional regulation or other areas that seemed stable.

It may also be anticlimactic. Your child may encounter the same issues as typical teens and you'll get to suffer through them like all the other parents.

If you see your teen struggling with new issues, talk to him or her about them. Your child may be aware of an issue but not know how to approach it, they may be fine with handling it the way they are, or the issue may not have made it onto their radar yet.

5. QUESTIONS?

Not yours, your child's. Keep the lines of communication open and emphasize that your son or daughter can ask you about anything, no matter how silly, strange, uncomfortable or obvious it might seem. If he or she has difficulty raising questions verbally (and this can be true even of tweens and teens that are usually verbal); offer the option to ask questions in writing and to receive the answers in writing as well. That way your youngster can reread them as often as necessary.

*

The tips here are by no means all-inclusive. They're simply the things that come to mind when I think about the kind of information that would have been helpful for me as I navigated the confusing years of puberty and adolescence.

If you're looking for additional information about how to talk with your autistic child about puberty, sexuality, and adolescent hygiene, http://www.autismhelp.info/teen-years/sexuality-puberty-and-hygiene/ is an excellent resource. The website also includes a nice set of visual aids you can download and use in talking with your child.

Bio: Cynthia Kim is the author of "I Think I Might Be Autistic: A Guide to Autism Spectrum Disorder Diagnosis and Self-Discovery for Adults". She blogs about her experiences as an adult with late-diagnosed ASD at Musings of an Aspie.

5

for the need to chew

Stylish   Discreet   Safe

Nail biter? Pencil Chewer? Hair Twirler? Fidgety Hands?

Stylish, FUNctional, jewelry designed to look amazing while discreetly serving the need to chew.

Designed for all ages, Chewigem can be worn as a discreet chewing aid.

Varying designs and colors allow there to be a special Chewigem for everyone!

SAVE 10% WITH CODE APM10

www.chewigem.com

Australasia ~ United Kingdom ~ United States

SOCIAL HELP

If You Could Talk to Your Teen Self

M. Kelter

> I was recently asked, "What advice would you give your teen self about friendship?" It was an interesting question to consider since I was diagnosed as being on the autism spectrum at the age of 30.

It was only then that I could look back and finally begin to make sense of my life. I had always struggled with non-verbal pragmatics, to such a degree that it created a variety of social delays. Even as a young child, I had a strong desire for connection with others, yet found the social world to be incomprehensible.

So this question adolescence and friendship gave me a chance to really think about the advice I needed to hear when I was growing up. I thought I would share those answers with you here. I was dealing with very different issues during early and later adolescence, so I will break my response to this question into two parts.

 IN MY EXPERIENCE, PRESSURING YOUNG PEOPLE ON THE SPECTRUM TO "CATCH UP" WITH OTHERS IN THEIR AGE GROUP CAN SERIOUSLY UNDERMINE THEIR CONFIDENCE AND SELF-ESTEEM.

From childhood up to the age of 15, the challenge for me was understanding the structure of social interactions. I didn't know how to begin and end conversations; I didn't understand the concept of "give and take". As a result of this, I made a habit of unintentionally breaking the unwritten rules of the social world. I tended to share ideas without providing context, for example. I would just walk up to classmates and launch into a description of whatever was on my mind in that moment. My goal was to connect with others, but the only result was that it pushed people away.

Once I entered junior high, my sense of alienation increased exponentially. I was consciously aware of the fact that other kids were forming friendships and cliques with ease. I was lonely, anxious to start making friends, and as a result of this pressure I often just tried too hard. I couldn't puzzle out how to successfully interact with people, so I tended to overcompensate by standing too close, talking too loud; actions that once again had the effect of pushing people away.

So if I could talk to myself during those early teen years, I would give advice based on these struggles. First of all, I needed to know that the unwritten rules of conversation even existed. It's a fact so obvious to most that no one ever thought to tell me. I would educate myself about basic communication tools that could help. For example, later in life I taught myself a lot of stock phrases that made it easier for me to navigate discussions; basic questions like, "How are you?" or "How's it going?" Again, these things are obvious for most people, yet I had to learn small talk piece by piece, as if it were a foreign language.

7

SOCIAL HELP

I do want to say: the goal of teaching social skills to children and teens on the spectrum should not be normalization. I think a better mindset is to think of social skills as a tool box; something that the child or teen can carry with them and use as needed. If they run into trouble, they can reach into that tool box and find something- like a phrase or gesture- that might help.

THE TRUTH IS MANY AUTISTICS HAVE A STRONG DESIRE FOR CONNECTION AND JUST DISCOVER A VARIETY OF BARRIERS ALONG THE WAY

In my experience, pressuring young people on the spectrum to "catch up" with others in their age group can seriously undermine their confidence and self-esteem. Therapies and supports can be great, but it's important that they be predicated on acceptance and respect for that person's unique personality. In short: help as needed, but don't force expectations. This is why, in my life, the "tool box" mentality has been useful. It allows me to employ a memorized skill as needed, without feeling a need to conceal my differences or hide who I am.

Beyond the age of 15, my social issues changed in nature, so my advice for that time period regarding friendship would be a little different. I was in high school at that point, a time when the pressure to fit in was at a fever pitch. If I could go back and say anything to myself then, it would be: "None of this pressure matters. Ignore it"

Easier said than done, but a message I needed to hear nonetheless. I found myself at the bottom of the social ladder in high school, and found it difficult to feel any sense of connection to the world. I definitely needed to know that the values my peers held in such high esteem- status, popularity, etc.- were actually frivolous, and would have no relevance as time went on. It's a lesson we all learn, eventually: popularity has an expiration date of high school graduation; after that, it evaporates and everyone gets a clean slate.

Individuals on the spectrum are just different. Their minds and senses can work in different ways, so it's important that those with unique perceptions not compare themselves to others. I needed to know this. I needed to understand that my differences allowed me to have more interesting thoughts and reactions. At that time, all I could see was that the world reacted to difference with ridicule, and rejection. I didn't know

SOCIAL HELP

then what I know now: differences are strengths. They save you from a conventional mindset that most people never have an opportunity to escape.

With so much pressure to hide differences, it's a challenge to build self-esteem and protect your sense of self. But that needed to be goal number one for me, during high school. My younger self could have benefited from learning a few social skills, but as time went on, I definitely needed a new skill set: confidence. Not over-confidence or arrogance. I just needed the ability to identify my strengths and weather the challenges that all teens face, especially those with neurological differences.

What does this have to do with friendship? Over time, I've learned that if you can feel good about the fact that you're different- that you're not superficial and can engage with people in more meaningful ways- it will make it a lot easier to connect with people who are interesting and more genuine. Conversely, if you're preoccupied with concepts like popularity and the reindeer games of high school, you can lose track of what really matters. My goal back then needed to be, not making a lot of friends, but making the *right* friends.

A common misconception is that people on the autism spectrum are "shut down;" not interested in other people. The truth is many autistics have a strong desire for connection and just discover a variety of barriers along the way; the largest barrier being the negative reaction many people have to those who seem different. This brings me back to the original question, "What would you say to your teen self about friendship?" I'd say everything I've listed above, and I would add: you are going to make friends in your life; you are going to connect with people; and you will accomplish these things, not in spite of your differences, but because of them.

> M. Kelter was diagnosed as being on the autism spectrum at the age of 30, after years of social isolation. He now writes about life on the spectrum, focusing on: childhood and adolescent experiences with mindblindness, depression, as well as his ongoing efforts to decode the social world. He is currently writing at Invisible Strings, and can also be found on Twitter and Facebook.

PRESS RELEASE

With Pet Owners' Help, Canines For Disabled Kids Will Receive Grant From Crazy Pet Children's Foundation's "1000 Points Of Love" Campaign

Sending In Dog Pictures To Fill Giant Heart Can Help Make A Disabled Child's Dream Of Having A Service Dog Come True

WORCESTER, MA – A dog can make a big difference in a kid's life — but having a canine companion can be a life-changing event for a child with a disability who gets paired with a trained service dog.

Matthew has Asperger's Syndrome, a condition that makes it difficult and terrifying to go out in public and interact with people. After he received his service dog, "Quincy," the 8-year-old started coming out of his shell and his precocious intelligence began to shine. "I love my dog because he helps me with a lot of things that sometimes I can't control," said Matt. "Sometimes I'm crying in a crowd, and Quincy helps me a ton by licking and kissing me so I feel better. He helps me talk to people."

Matt and Quincy were brought together by Canines for Disabled Kids (CDK), a non-profit Worcester, MA-based organization that helps disabled children across the US connect with dogs that can assist them in their daily lives - whether it's turning on lights, picking up objects, or simply making them feel less alone and scared. Given their own special four-legged "helper," children with autism, hearing impairments,

SOCIAL HELP

paralysis and a variety of other disabilities have overcome their limitations and gone on to lead independent and confident lives.

But, unfortunately, many service dog programs don't accept kids under 18, which is why CDK was started. The group works with service dog training organizations around the country, such as Canine Partners For Life, to find the perfect canine companion for children with a wide range of disabilities.

Since its founding in 1998, the organization has helped pair more than 130 service dogs with young people like Matthew and wheelchair-bound teenager Erica, another of the organization's many stellar success stories.

Before canine friend "Baker" came into her life, Erica's ambitions of going to college and studying marine biology seemed like a far-fetched dream. Her family was concerned about the safety risks that Erica's desire for an independent lifestyle would expose her to. Not only did the fluffy Golden Retriever help Erica with tasks like opening doors, he became her constant protector, riding along on the school bus every day and going shopping with her at the mall. When Erica graduated from high school (with Baker proudly at her side), the best friends embarked on the next phase of their adventure together, heading off to college!

As part of its mission to bring child-canine teams together, CDK offers scholarships to help defray the cost of training a service dog. Families are typically expected to pay an average of $12,000$15,000 of the $25,000 it costs to train a service dog. With many families already saddled with medical expenses, this was often more than they could afford.

Now CDK has an angel-benefactor of its own. Cardinal Pet Care, a Los Angeles-based pet product manufacturer, has chosen the organization to be the recipient of a grant from its charitable Crazy Pet Children's Foundation's (CPFC) 1,000 Points Of Love fund-raising campaign. The company has posted a giant heart on its website www.cardinalpetcare.com/heart , which it hopes to fill with pictures of dogs sent in by their owners. CPFC will donate $1 for each dog picture it receives and then award a $1,000 grant to CDK once the heart gets filled with 1,000 photos, thus the campaign's name -"1000 Points Of Love."

A unique feature of the 1000 Points Of Love campaign is that it doesn't ask for monetary donations, it just requests that people email a photo of their dog. Barbara Denzer, Cardinal Pet Care's vice president, explained why: "We wanted to give people a chance to contribute to this great cause without asking for money. Sending a picture of your dog is such a visible way to show kids we care about them. Photos of pets are a far more personal and emotional donation. The project is a great way to support Canines For Disabled Kids."

"This support is so important to helping children come together with the perfect service dog. These funds will go a long way in helping to bring another child and service dog together," says Kristin Hartness, CDK's executive director.

Pet owners can help by sending a picture of their dog (or their friend or neighbor's dog) to "mailto:news@cardinalpet.com">news@cardinalpet.com .. The pictures will be used to create a giant heart-shaped poster. For more information go to www.CaninesForKids.org

The Crazy Pet Children's Foundation's grant program was established in 2009 by Cardinal Pet Care CEO Tony de Vos to support groups that teach children about pet care and strengthen bonds between animals and young people. Learn more about the Crazy Pet Children's Foundation at www.cardinalpet.com/foundation/index.html

Charis Hills

Summer Camp

For Children With Learning Differences

HF Autism • ADD/HD • LD • Asperger's

Charis Hills is a Christian recreational and educational summer camp for children with learning and social difficulties. Our campers discover a highly personalized, fun-filled and nurturing environment while filling their heart's desire to be accepted and succeed in new activities.

www.charishills.org

Toll-Free (888) 681-2173

CARING & SHARING CHRIST WITH HIS KIDS

OT ADVICE

Not Only a Powerful Tool for Health Professionals, But Also Parents of Autistic Children

By: Bill Wong, OTD, OTR/L

Pinterest is becoming one of the most popular social media platforms since its inception a few years ago. People use it to pin various things- wedding ideas, food recipes, fashion ideas, funny things, etc. For many allied health professionals and students in these fields (such as occupational therapy, physical therapy, and speech therapy), Pinterest has become a place for them to collect their treatment ideas for the clients they are going to see now or in the future.

I first started on Pinterest in early 2012 at the recommendation of one of my ex-classmates from occupational therapy school. I decided to join after she wrote a blog about its benefits. I then started to follow whoever I am connected to on Twitter and Facebook who also has Pinterest. As I began to see pins (pictures with captions of what the links for the pins are about) of occupational therapy related things, I was like, "Where was this a few years ago?" So, I have been collecting pins left and right. In terms of autism ideas, I can find anything from sensory activities, to behavior management strategies, to fine motor and gross motor activities, to possible apps I can use during treatment.

I originally started with one big occupational therapy board. However, because it became too big, I had to separate out to different areas of occupational therapy practice. I also was not content with just people I know on social media. So, I followed more people on it if I found out that they are also in the occupational therapy profession. Two years later, I have over 11,000 pins combined on occupational therapy related stuff.

Why do you have to care, you may ask? The more allied health professionals or students you follow on Pinterest, the higher probability that you will get quality information on autism and better understand what the professionals are doing. After all, these students or professionals most likely will weed out information that might not be helpful for them. Also, some of them have really organized Pinterest boards. Although these pins won't constitute as health professional advice, it is very useful for you to check out these links and see if there are things you can use for your children at home or as suggestions for the allied health professionals you work with.

My overall advice with Pinterest- If an app is suggested for your iPad or iPhone, please consult your children's professionals first. They may have an idea on whether the app is appropriate for your children as well as what will be a just right challenge for them. If the professionals don't have the answer right away, you can ask other parents online before you decide on an app and then ask questions to the professionals if necessary. When you do the latter, however, please try out the

OT ADVICE

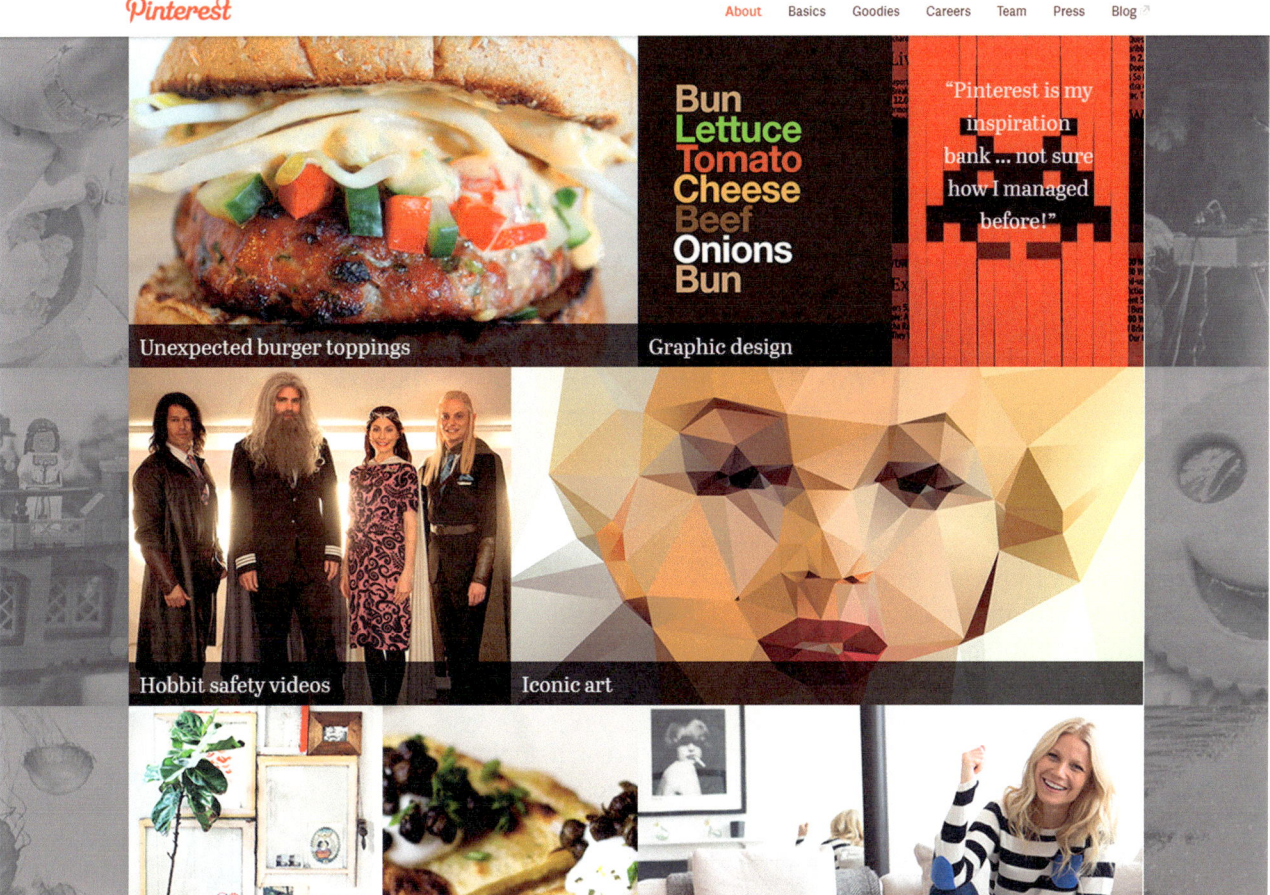

app first and anticipate how your children might perform. This preparation is important because you have to determine whether it is adequate to meet your children's needs.

For other things, please read thoroughly of what the links provide and determine whether the information is useful for your children. Also, you have to determine whether you have the means to set up or purchase the necessary items. If you are unsure, please ask a professional on your children's care team who most likely can answer the question for clarifications.

I am not saying Pinterest can replace online or offline autism support groups. However, it can give you more ideas in case you are running out of them if you are not sure of what to do for your children. That said, with each pin you collect on Pinterest in regards to autism, I highly suggest you check out each site individually.

You can find Autism Parenting on Pinterest at http://www.pinterest.com/autismparentmag/

BIO:

Bill is a licensed occupational therapist in California. He is planning to make a transition to become an autism life coach. He received his masters and clinical doctorate degrees in occupational therapy from University of Southern California in 2011 and 2013, respectively. He is believed to be the first autistic individual in the world to receive a doctorate degree of any kind in occupational therapy, as he was diagnosed with Asperger's Syndrome in 2010. Bill has presented 8 times in local, national, and international occupational therapy conferences. He also was a guest on American Occupational Therapy Association (AOTA)'s Pediatrics Virtual Chat, and Autism Live web show, OT Go To podcast. His immediate professional goal is to be part of the AOTA's Emerging Leaders Program within the next two years. His long term professional goal is to be an AOTA fellow and deliver an Eleanor Slagle Lecture at a future AOTA conference.

LIFE SKILLS

Engaging the Community of a Child with Autism:
The Why, Who and How

By Michael J. Cameron, PhD, BCBA-D, Pacific Child and Family Associates

WHEN IT COMES TO LEARNING NEW SKILLS, CHILDREN ON THE AUTISM SPECTRUM NEED MORE OPPORTUNITIES TO LEARN AND ENGAGE.

One of the best ways to do that is by involving other important people in the child's life – parents, grandparents, siblings and other caregivers – and incorporating their skills and interests into the natural rhythms of a child's day. With a "strength-based approach," meaning the practice or strategy in identifying and drawing upon the strength and interests of an individual, their family, and community to achieve engagement and results as a partner, families can achieve an established goal set out for a child with autism.

By focusing on activities that family members already enjoy and naturally gravitate towards, it increases the likelihood that the important skills you are hoping to achieve will be addressed. For example, if the son's Grandma loves to bake and sees the child once or twice per week, during their time together Grandma can help the son with a baking project (something she loves) so that he can get experience in social communication skills (something he needs).

The benefits of this approach include:

- Using authentic materials in the context of familiar environments.
- Capitalizing on naturally occurring consequences.
- Increasing a child's exposure to opportunities and approaches.
- Maintaining and developing functional skills used across different settings.

Follow these steps to create a plan that will work for your child's needs as well as family members.

Start with a list of the child's needs.

The process starts with the child's needs. First, gather together a list of their specific needs in development, based on their Individualized Education Program (IEP) or standardized assessment tools. Write down the specific skills they'll need to practice which may include:

- Language and communication (i.e., touching a person to get attention, pointing to items when requested)
- Fine motor skills (e.g., using scissors, turning dials)
- Gross motor skills (e.g., walking up and down stairs)

LIFE SKILLS

- Adaptive skills (e.g., using silverware, dressing and undressing)
- Social communication skills (e.g., following multiple-step directions)
- Cognitive skills (e.g., retelling an event in sequence)
- Social skills (e.g., working cooperatively in a small group)

Identify the interests of family members and caregivers.

Make a list of the people involved and their skill sets and interests. For example, a cousin may be a talented musician and willing to work with the child once a month on rhythm and music games. A babysitter may be a part-time gymnastics instructor and can assist with physical coordination development. Anyone that takes interest in or has an active caretaking role with the child should be considered.

Create a matrix to match personal interests to skill instruction.

Use the lists you've created to develop a matrix. An example is given below. The matrix will display the individuals that will spend time with the child, their skills and interests, and how each of those interests ties into the assessment-driven goals and objectives.

With the matrix in hand, you can reach out to the aunt that rides horses or the sibling who loves to design board games and ask for their assistance in developing a specific skill. It gives everyone a choice, and a level of control, on a child's activities and how they spend time with that child.

It's important to lay down expectations with the family members and caregivers. Explain to them how their natural talents and interests can help the child, but keep expectations within line with personal capacity. You don't want to overwhelm the caregiver with extra responsibilities. Emphasize that by doing their favorite things with the child, it will help them develop their skills and have new opportunities.

Keep in mind that a matrix isn't static. It creates a good starting point for maximizing experiences for a child and getting others involved in positive, constructive ways. However, regular updates and fine-tuning may be needed to avoid boredom, emphasize different skills, or accommodate changes. It can take 40 days to form a habit, so give yourself, the family members, and the child enough time to adjust and make changes as you see fit.

Family members often feel powerless and like they are relying on professionals to guide their child in their skills development. With this approach, the whole family – related or not – can get involved. It gives them the tools to be empowered and help with a child's development, without demanding that they reach too far outside of their comfort zone.

ABOUT DR. MICHAEL J. CAMERON
Dr. Michael J. Cameron, a Board Certified Behavior Analyst® (Charter Certificant 1-00-0010) is The Chief Clinical Officer for Pacific Child and Family Associates (PCFA) and experienced in the area of behavioral medicine, behavioral health assessment, intervention for diverse populations, and higher education. Prior to joining PCFA, Dr. Cameron was a tenured Associate Professor and the Founding Chair of the Department of Behavior Analysis at Simmons College. Dr. Cameron earned a master's degree in applied behavior analysis and a Ph.D. in experimental psychology from Northeastern University.

SKILLS MATRIX

Support Person	Interests	Activity	Fine Motor	Gross Motor	Language	Social	Adaptive
Nana	• Cooking • Kayaking	• Baking • River Trip	• Cut dough with scissors • Adjust straps on life vest	• Use rolling pin • Paddle kayak	• Request more dough to cut • Label items on the shore	• Bring baked goods to people • Greet other boaters	• Wash hands • Clear boat, return paddles and vests
Dad	• Hiking • Model airplane flying	• Nature walk • Trip to the airfield	• Pick up acorns • Lower landing gear on plane	• Step up on rocks • Run to retrieve plane after landing	• Request trail mix • Request to fly and handle controls	• Talk to other hikers • Comment about other's airplanes	• Use public restroom • Dress for flying

15

The Son-Rise Program®
of the Autism Treatment Center of America

Providing you with new techniques to reach your child.
You're not giving up on your child. Neither will we.

Let us help you.
- We are a caring, respectful relationship-based alternative to ABA.
- We've had a record of success for over 35 years in 90 countries worldwide.
- We'll build your confidence, optimism, and ability to interact with your child.
- We'll help you customize the techniques to your child's specific needs (high or low functioning, 2 years old through adulthood).
- Learn to join your child in their own special world - and show them how to join you in yours.
- Help your child learn without you having to push or pressure.

AWARDED National AutismOne Conference Best Autism Therapy

Looking for a new direction for your child?
Speak to a *Son-Rise Program Advisor* and get all your questions answered.

**Email: psupport@option.org,
Call: 413-229-3202 USA,
         001-413-229-2100 International**

**Be sure to mention
*Autism Parenting Magazine***

"We enrolled him in our state's early intervention, the whole mainstream route. We went ABA and noticed he began to become very aggressive, irritable, untrusting, and rigid and much more repetitive. We attended The Son-Rise Program Start-Up and within the first week our son transformed so much. He went from rigid and miserable and tantrums; not a happy child to now trusting and loving us. He runs over into my arms. Two months ago I couldn't have him hold my hand without him having a full blown tantrum."

*Leah K., Connecticut, Son: Noam, Age 4,
Diagnosis: Autism*

NEWS

A NEW YEAR, AND HOPE FOR CHANGE

By Megan Kelly

As 2013 has drawn to a close, and with the Holiday season behind us, it's time for 2014 to begin in earnest. For many people the beginning of a new year presents an opportunity for productive or positive personal change.

Many individuals make New Year Resolutions, or set goals or promises to better themselves, or their environment, in the New Year to come. Some vow to try new things that would benefit themselves or others around them.

For many in the autism community, both those with autism themselves, and those with autistic loved ones, 2014 is offering hope for a beginning of change in the way that society views autism. It may also bring about the possibility of a change in how those affected with autism can get financial assistance, as well as positive and helpful education related to their conditions. Some of this change centers around sponsors, and those that donate their time and money to organizations, and charities that support people with autism. The organizations use this money to conduct research, educate the public, and offer financial help and equipment to those that need it.

In 2013 a boycott and petition was started against Autism Speaks, one of the most well known, though not necessarily well loved, autism organizations. Although Autism

17

Speaks has many corporate and private sponsors, a number of whom donate large amounts of money to them, recent events and data have shown that perhaps this is not the most beneficial organization for companies, or individuals to be donating to. Autism Speaks claims to offer support through financial and educational resources to those with autism, and their families. Yet if one looks at the data for Autism Speaks, it raises some serious questions about where the money donated to the organization is actually being used. Data from the 2012 audited financial reports of Autism Speaks (2013 data is not yet available), can be viewed on Charitynavigator.org

Charitynavigator.org is well known website that provides financial data and ratings for many different charities, and organizations. This gives potential donors the ability to see exactly where their money is being used in a charity that they have decided to donate to. The websites data shows that Autism Speaks earns only 1 out of 4 stars for their financial expenditures. "We believe that those spending less than a third of their budget on program expenses are simply not living up to their missions. Our data shows that 7 out of 10 charities we've evaluated spend at least 75% of their budget on the programs, and services they exist to provide. And 9 out of 10 spend at least 65%." The data shows that Autism Speaks spends only a very small amount on family services, grants, and awards. This leaves one to wonder why they make so many claims about helping, and donating to those with autism that need assistance. More information about this can be found on http://www.charitynavigator.org, as well as http://www.boycottautismspeaks.com.

The list of corporate sponsors of Autism Speaks is a long one. Well-known companies such as Toys R Us, Build a Bear, Shop Rite, GAP, FedEx, Home Depot, and Zale's are all large companies, and they support and sponsor Autism Speaks. Perhaps 2014 will be the year that these companies can sit down, and really take a good look at the organizations that they are donating their money to. Hopefully they will become aware of the recent petition and boycott, and it will help to influence their decision about whether or not to continue their support.

Although the restaurant chain Panera Bread is still listed on Autism Speaks website as being a corporate sponsor, we recently contacted Jonathan Yohannan, the director of public relations via email. Jonathan

9 out of 10 charities SPEND AT LEAST 65% of their budget on the programs

was kind enough to set up a phone conversation to discuss autism in general, as well as give an answer to the question of whether or not the company he works for would be continuing to support Autism Speaks in 2014. Jonathan stated that

"Our corporate focus is on fighting food insecurity. However, franchisees have the flexibility to support a variety of causes locally and nationally including the important issue of autism. As of today, we are not aware of any planned campaigns that support Autism Speaks in 2014."

Although Panera Bread has not joined the boycott, or signed the petition against Autism Speaks, it was encouraging to learn that a company as large as Panera was concerned enough about the issue, as well as about autism in general, to respond to our inquiries, and the concerns that many in the autism community have about Autism Speaks. Hopefully more of the companies that support Autism Speaks will continue doing research, and look a little more closely at the current statistics and data, before continuing to donate to an organization that does not appear to be doing much help or good for those that they claim to support.

There is hope that this New Year may turn out to be one full of better education, better and more readily available assistance, and acceptance by society concerning autism. If sponsors do their research, and look into the reasons behind the boycott of Autism Speaks, they may well find out that their money would be better donated elsewhere. By donating to organizations that spend more of their money on directly helping those with autism, the sponsors will be helping to better individual lives, better educate society, provide support for those who need it, and condone acceptance and equality for everyone.

Sources
http://www.charitynavigator.org
http://www.boycottautismspeaks.com
http://www.change.org

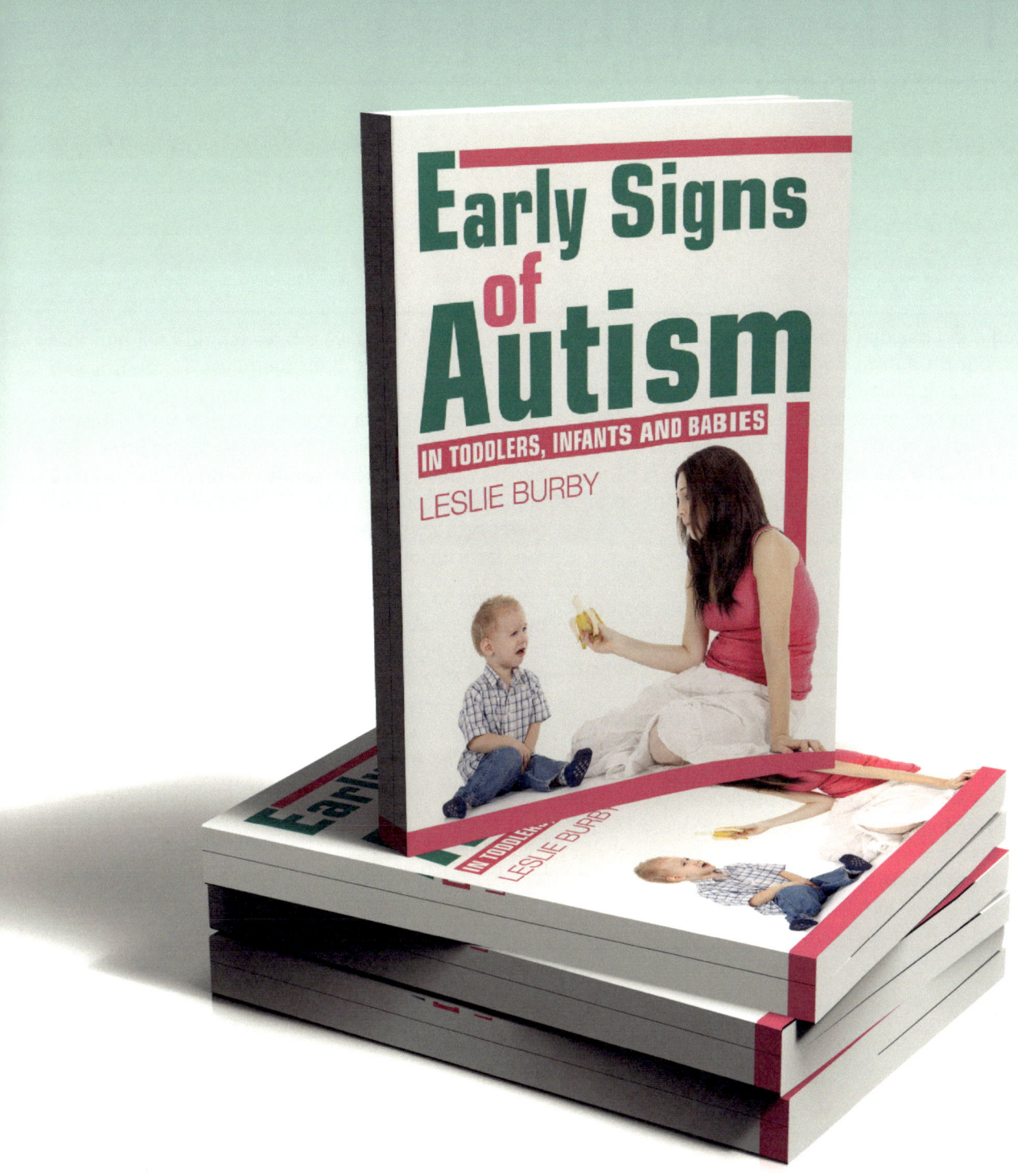

AutismParentingMagazine.com/EarlySignsPB

PARENTAL POISE

"The Autism Talk"

Kimberlee Rutan McCafferty

"When I was a little boy did I have autism?" my smallest son asks as he pauses momentarily in his teeth brushing duties. I feel my heart skip a beat as I realize this is "the moment," followed by the thought chaser that his father isn't home, and I'll be handling this myself.

Jeff and I decided years ago to wait to tell Zach about his autism until he started asking questions, and privately I decided to also wait until my mommy gut told me the time was right. That tiny voice which has been both my solace and saving grace all these years tells me this is my chance, in the quiet confines of our guest bathroom, to tell him.

It's time for the "autism talk."

I wrap his Thomas the Train towel more securely around his tall but lithe figure, and settle him down on my lap. I tell him when he was eighteen months old he got sick, had a high fever for days, was miserable. I tell him that after that illness he seemed to lose his words, was relegated to a vocabulary of "mama" and "juice" that bore no resemblance to his formerly loquacious self. I share with him that loose bowels tormented him for weeks until we removed gluten from his diet, and that in time, his tummy slowly healed, his words returned, as did the light in his eyes that had so entranced us. I tell him that a doctor told us he had a "little autism," not a lot like his brother, but a little all the same.

He asks me if he'll always have it, and I tell him that most people have it all of their lives. He pauses and processes, and after this momentary break I remind him his brother has it too. I tell him that autism is what enabled Justin to read at the tender age of three. I tell him it's what makes him so smart, and so creative. I tell him that autism gave him the gift of a phenomenal memory, it's what enables him to retain all the dinosaur facts he loves so well.

I proceed to regale him again with stories of famous people presumed to have autism, ranging from contemporary figures to geniuses of the past like Albert Einstein, Mozart, and Thomas Jefferson. I share with him once more the fantastic contributions they have made to the world, that like Mozart and Michelangelo he loves and excels at music and art as well. I tell him that autism is what helps make him so unique and special, that his family loves him, that so many people love him. I tell him for the thousandth time how in awe I am of him, how my heart fills with pride that he tries

PARENTAL POISE

so hard every day to conquer his fears and challenges. He hugs me and responds with exuberance that he will write a letter to George Lucas the next day and ask for a list of all the Star Wars characters who have autism.

Perhaps someone can help me out with finding his address.

After his George Lucas declaration he bounds from the bathroom to his bedroom to select his favorite pajamas, and I remain seated momentarily, allow myself to catch my breath after this momentous moment. I can hear that he's moved on in his thought processes and is composing a story about dinosaurs without autism, and that the window on this topic has shut for now, but remains wedged open. I think back over all the years I've been building to this moment, the times my husband and I have touted Justin's innate intelligence, his affectionate nature, all the wonderful traits that this child with autism possesses in spades. My mind wanders to all the discussions we've had about contributions made by autistic people, how smart they often are, how innovative. My son selects this moment to run in to ask me if there were kids in his pre-school with autism, and when I respond in the affirmative, he tells me that I'd put him in the right place.

Not only did this talk go well, I get validation. This is quickly becoming my favorite conversation ever.

Soon his father comes home, and I quickly sneak in that we've had "the talk" before he enters Zach's bedroom, and before my husband has the chance to take it all in, my son yells "Daddy, I have a little autism!" and throws himself on his father, wrapping torso and limbs tightly around my spouse's still-moving legs. Jeff looks at me and mouths "That went well," and I smile in response, and try to corral an excited six-year-old to bed. On this night he asks me to cuddle with him as I read him his story, and I happily comply, as now that he is a "medium boy" I am not always invited for this treat. Soon kisses are dispensed, and I prepare myself that he may not capitulate to the onslaught of sleep, that all of this information may compel him to leave his bed on several occasions.

Several? Let's make that six.

I head downstairs for that glass of wine I've rightly deserved, at peace with my declaration, enthralled with how it went down. My smallest son has autism. He knows it now, and our talk could not have gone better. His reaction was elation, coupled with pride, chased with joy at the gifts his autism will bring to him.

And as I banish forever all the years of fear that have led up to this moment, I couldn't be more proud myself.

Bio: I'm the mom of two young sons on the autism spectrum, ages six and ten. I'm a former educator, and presently a stay-at-home mom/therapist. I've been published in Exceptional Parent Magazine, and my blog, http://autismmommytherapist.wordpress.com/, is linked to multiple sites throughout the country on *Patch*, an online source for community-specific news. Last year I produced and directed a play about mothers raising autistic children, with all proceeds going directly to POAC Autism Services, a non-profit located in Brick, NJ. All profits from my book, "*Raising Autism*" will go directly to Autism Speaks, Parents of Autistic Children (POAC), Someone Special Needs You (SSNY), and my son's school. Connect with me on Facebook at Autism Mommy-Therapist.

BOOK SECTION

AUTISM AND THE WORLD ACCORDING TO MATT

Liz Becker

MOTHER'S BEST-SELLING MEMOIR CHRONICLES AUTISTIC SON'S REMARKABLE JOURNEY FROM DIAGNOSIS TO INDEPENDENT LIVING

Liz Becker's inspiring new book uses a collection of uplifting short stories to depict Matt's gifted first 25 years of life that beat all odds. As one of the few grassroots books written about a child with severe and mostly non-verbal Autism, 'Autism and the World According to Matt' is making compelling reading for any parent, educator or medical professional.

Wytheville, Virginia – When Matt was diagnosed with severe Autism in the 1980s, the future was laid out in front of him and mother Liz Becker – a life requiring full-time help that would lead to eventual institutionalization. However, following twenty-five testing yet hugely-fulfilling years, Matt has joined most other men his age by enjoying the joys and freedom of independent living – a feat that is almost non-existent among those living with the severe condition.

Having learned from Matt as much as he learned from her, Liz Becker has compiled their touching and uplifting journey into a heartfelt new book of short stories, titled 'Autism and the World According to Matt'.

Abridged synopsis:

Autism and the World According to Matt is a collection of inspirational short stories about a moderate to severe and mostly non-verbal autistic child and his journey from diagnosis to living independently. The collection covers 25 years of milestones and insights into the difficulties in communication, socialization, and understanding. It offers insights into how to teach and learn from such a unique individual. The milestones are many, as Matt was diagnosed in the 1980s, when autism was a rare disorder with very little information on how it affects behavior and cognition. Specialists recommended institutionalization….but that wasn't what his mother saw in his future. She saw hope, and talent and an ability to learn.

As a scientist, Matt's mom was naturally curious about his behaviors and sought the meaning behind everything from the appearance of "a world of his own" to sensory overload and meltdowns. She wanted to see what her son saw, feel what he felt and as she looked deeper she gained understanding and insight into her son.

Matt became the first autistic child to enter the area school system in a regular classroom, and teachers were skeptical of the very idea. To everyone's amazement, Matt graduated near the top of his class - no one could predict what he could achieve after high school. Although his severity prevents him from having a job he still amazes family, friends, and professionals as he transitions to his "ultimate goal" – a home of his very own – something rare among autistic individuals on the severe end of the spectrum.

Liz Becker hopes that her own story will provide vital hope to other parents fighting the daily battle and perceived constraints of autism.

"Matt achieved everything that doctors, care staff and society-at-large said was impossible. I want other parents to understand there is hope for their own child to do the same. Each story in this book is accompanied by an inspirational message of interacting, learning and ultimately – understanding," says Becker, who frequently speaks to parental support groups.

Reviews for the book have been extremely positive. For example, reader Bryan comments, "A must read for teachers, parents, siblings or anyone who is interested

BOOK SECTION

S. Keller was equally as impressed, adding, "Autism can be like a country without a map. Liz Becker has trekked through the world of autism with Matt. Her collection of essays is enlightening and encouraging."

'Autism and the World According to Matt' is available now: http://amzn.to/1e9DcoT. For more information, visit: https://www.facebook.com/autismrevealed.

About the Author:

Liz Becker has been promoting autism awareness for 25 years, and her website, "World According to Matt" (http:// worldaccordingtomatt.com) won Top 30 Autism Blogs for Parents in 2012 award from Babble, and currently reaches 84 countries around the world with nearly 4 million "Facebook Likes".

She is an Associate Instructor for Wytheville Community College, and adjunct Instructor for Radford University where she teaches Anatomy and Physiology, Biology and Microbiology.

in autism. Becker balances the insight and curiosity of a scientist with the love and compassion that only a mother knows."

 # Helping Hands Art and Exercise

Providing opportunities for individuals with autism and other developmental disabilities.

A unique FITNESS DVD specifically created for people with autism
"MOVE WITH US"
$21.99

- For all ages and abilities. Features easy-to-follow repetitive moves and upbeat music.

- Rhythmic counting to keep people engaged. It's exercising, it's dancing, it's fun! Use MOVE WITH US with your child. Not only do you get special time with your child, but everyone benefits from the healthy exercise!

- Dr. Coury writes, "Exercise can be good for children with autism and may help improve problem behaviors. Benefits from exercise can last for several hours during and after exercise."

To order go to www.HelpingHandsArt.com or Amazon.com

Reach Out

We encourage you to send in your questions, comments, suggestions and concerns to AutismParenting@gmail.com. We will do our best to find you answers, resources, and improve the magazine to help all families with children on the autism spectrum. Please note that we may post your questions and edit them if needed. Please include a phone number in case we need clarification. We thank you for reaching out to us. We will do our best to provide helpful resources and the most current information.

Q: I have a daughter that is ten with autism and I don't know how to explain or talk to her about when girls get their monthly period. I am worried how my daughter will react when she gets her first period.

A: Many parents with children on the spectrum, as well as most parents with typical children, have problems with talking to their children about puberty and the beginning of menstruation. So many parents see their children as innocent and these parents have fears of destroying that innocence by revealing what society considers adult issues to the child. Unfortunately, this leads to seriously dangerous consequences. Every girl needs to know and has a right to know everything about her body and how it works. This does not take away her innocence, it protects her from disease, predators, and other societal dangers while at the same time empowers her to know what it truly means to be a woman, what her body can do, and when it is appropriate to talk about certain topics and allow others into her personal space.

The first thing any parent must do is to educate himself/herself on puberty, sexual maturation, and the pre-teen and teen social environments. You cannot give your child accurate information if you do not know enough yourself. Did you know that most adult women (all women, not just those on the spectrum) do not know the correct terms for their sexual organs? For example, many women do not know that the vulva is the external area of the female genitals, whereas the vagina is the internal tubular tract of the female genitals. They are two separate sex organs. Likewise, slang terminology and vague references such as "down there" should never be used when talking about female sex organs or sex in general unless used as examples of other things people may say so that the child is familiar with and aware of what others may be discussing around her or with her at any given time.

Next, after the parent educates herself and makes sure she has all the answers (or knows where to find the answers) to possible questions her daughter may have for her during a discussion, she can then go on and casually ask her daughter what she knows about puberty and if she knows what a girl's period or menstrual cycle is. The parent may be surprised with what her daughter already knows, and surprised at the possible misconceptions her daughter may have. Initially, parents should talk about the mechanics; every month a girl goes through a menstrual cycle where the uterine lining is shed, (pictures and examples should be shown to illustrate.) This information can be readily obtained via the internet, of course monitored first by the parent before showing the information to the child.

During any discussion about puberty, menstruation, or sex the parent should be calm, cheerful, and show no signs of anxiety or stress. All children, even those on the spectrum, pick up on this. Menstruation is not scary, it is not horrible and it should not be treated as such. It should be treated as normal, natural, and something every woman shares. After describing the mechanics the daughter needs to be shown and given options for cleanliness. The proper use of pads, tampons, and how to properly wash herself throughout her period should be demonstrated and shown to her long

Q&A SECTION

before her menstrual cycle begins. She needs to be well prepared ahead of time. You want her to learn these behaviors from you the parent, not a teacher, school nurse, or stranger. For those on the spectrum surprises are not usually welcome, if she is well prepared and knows exactly what to do when her period occurs, she will most likely be perfectly fine.

Additionally, another important thing to discuss is when it is appropriate for the daughter to talk about her period and body changes. For instance, she needs to be explicitly told that she should not raise her hand in class to "change a tampon" but to simple raise her hand and ask to use the restroom. Many on the spectrum do not know what needs to be kept private and what is open knowledge. She needs to be told this directly. Bodily functions in our society must be handled discreetly. This needs to be taught explicitly, clearly, and thoroughly. Furthermore, since the parent will be having a discussion about the child's body it is also the perfect time to talk about appropriate and inappropriate touch, and what to do if she isn't sure. The child is to be told directly using the correct words where she can and can't be touched. A safe bet is telling her that no one is allowed to touch anything her clothing covers with the exceptions being few and listed.

To summarize, the key points are to give the child as much accurate knowledge as possible so that her classmates and other people she comes in contact with do not give her inaccurate information, to explain exactly what menstruation is and its purpose in blunt and proper terms, to show her how to remain clean and hygienic during her menstrual cycle and be assured that she can handle this on her own without her parent's presence, appropriate times to discuss sexuality, and finally what is and isn't appropriate physical contact. All of this must be accomplished, and as soon as possible. Remember, this discussion does not have to take place all at once. Spread it out over a week or two because no child (autistic or not) can hold attention and process all of that information in one conversation. Also, don't feel that your job is done after the talk is over. The lines of communication must always remain open. The parent should always ask questions and provide additional age appropriate information about sexuality as her daughter gets older. If the parent is unsure about certain things she herself must educate herself before speaking with her daughter, or better yet research the topic together!

https://www.youtube.com/watch?v=ZvPVyas68jE
http://www.barbaradoyle.com/documents/SocialSexualSafetyBehaviorChecklist.pdf
http://www.barbaradoyle.com/documents/TenEssentialSkillsforaSafeandIndependentLife.pdf
http://www.barbaradoyle.com/documents/SafetyInSociety.pdf
http://www.amazon.com/Deal-Whole-Approach-Your-Brain/dp/0671041576/ref=sr_1_1?ie=UTF8&qid=1389026728&sr=8-1&keywords=deal+with+it
http://www.amazon.com/gp/offer-listing/0671041576

Q: Should I discuss puberty with my son?

A: Yes, discuss puberty with boys on the Autism Spectrum

While boys do not go through a reproductive cycle like menstruation when puberty arrives, they still experience changes that can be significant and difficult for the child and parent to handle. Just like girls, the best course of action is to make sure boys are properly prepared for puberty ahead of time. Boys are not immune from disease, predators, and societal dangers. In fact, sometimes they can inadvertently be labeled as predators themselves if they are not properly educated in what is and is not appropriate contact and behavior with others. Puberty brings on instincts and desires that the child may naturally seek out (because it feels good), and to have information prior to these feelings and hormones coming into play will greatly reduce any problems for the future.

Typically, boys start puberty a little later than girls and one of the first changes is an increase in testicle size, penis size, and pubic hair growth. Those on the spectrum need to know it is safe to talk about these changes with a parent, but not with a stranger. These rules need to be learned before

25

puberty, so that the child knows exactly what to do and who to talk to when he begins noticing changes with his body. Additionally, the increase of body hair and sweat glands calls for a discussion on hygiene and the importance of cleanliness. This issue is a common one for those on the spectrum, but where a child may be able to get away without bathing for a few days, a teenager will quickly develop odors that others may notice and find offensive. If there is an odor there is bacteria present and boys are not immune to bacterial skin infections, yeast infections, or other potentially serious consequences of not keeping clean. Teaching cleanliness before puberty begins is ideal so that hormones and defiant behaviors are not getting in the way of forming good hygiene habits.

The second change a boy notices is the ability to masturbate to ejaculation. Sometimes boys go through what is called "spontaneous erections" where there is no stimulus present to cause the erection. This can be scary or confusing to a child who has never experienced it before, and on the other end of the spectrum a child may not feel any embarrassment and begin to masturbate or display his erections in public. Before puberty begins parents must make sure their son understands that he must keep the action of masturbating private. A good way to help this process along before puberty is to teach the child to be clothed at all times except when bathing and alone in their room. Many parents with children on the spectrum have a hard time keeping clothes on their children due to sensory issues. Unfortunately, they then become teenagers running around naked. It is extremely difficult (but not impossible) to teach a teenager with a surge in hormones and defiant behaviors to put on clothes after spending years getting accustomed to the opposite. This must be taught before puberty and the concept that the penis must be covered and kept private a priority. This is important to discuss about others as well. It is not appropriate for a person to touch another person in their genital area. Children do not know this unless they are taught, and an autistic child may need to be taught this rule much more explicitly and completely in order for the rule to be learned and followed appropriately.

Furthermore, ejaculate must also be explained, similar to explaining the purpose of menstruation in girls. The biology and purpose of ejaculate needs to be described and understood so that the child knows the great power, responsibility, and reason for his erections. It is very important for a man to understand his role in reproduction, and again no slang terms should be used unless as an example of what others may say. The child must learn the correct terminology for all of his sexual organs and their functions. Additionally, banning masturbation is not going to keep your child from masturbating. In fact, it may simply increase the allure of the act. They must know how to do so in a cleanly way and dispose of the ejaculate properly. You would not let your child urinate on the floor, and they should not ejaculate on the floor either. The child must be taught that it is okay to masturbate privately but not when others are present, and if he chooses to do so privately he must clean himself properly just as he would after using the bathroom.

Lastly, most boys experience what is called a "wet dream." This is when the penis becomes erect and ejaculates during sleep. It is completely normal but surprising to a child who never experienced one before. They need to be warned that this could happen and what to do when it does. It is not something to be afraid of or embarrassed about. It simply means that the child's body is growing into a new stage of development. No child should ever be shamed for masturbating or having a wet dream. This can cause serious psychological distress. Everything relating to sexual development should be dealt with calmly, completely, and without judgment. You would not yell at your child while potty training, and you do not yell at your child while they are essentially training to become an adult.

Remember, it can take a long time for puberty to reach its conclusion. For those on the spectrum who are resistant to change, puberty can be a very long and distressing time full of various bodily changes. The best way to ease the child's transition into an adult body is preparation, communication, and patience. Give your child as much detailed knowledge about puberty as possible before he enters puberty, provide him with the purpose of puberty and why all children go through it, give him the opportunity to discuss and ask questions about his body without any feelings of discomfort or shame, and be patient with the frustrating behaviors that may come about during this time including: aggression, defiance, and emotional outbursts. For those on the spectrum these feelings are difficult to recognize and describe, so you the parent must help them interpret what they are going through and give them the tools they need to make it through as smoothly as possible.

Books on Puberty and Autism
http://www.amazon.com/Taking-Care-Myself-Personal-Curriculum/dp/1885477945/
http://www.amazon.com/Autism-Aspergers-Sexuality-Puberty-Jerry-Newport/dp/1885477880/

Male Puberty
http://science.howstuffworks.com/life/human-biology/male-puberty.htm

Puberty in boys
https://www.youtube.com/watch?v=X0folKJIBPU

Autism Parenting Tip: Make a Photobook
https://www.youtube.com/watch?v=DOHmhICDwR8

Jaclyn Hunt is a Certified Autism Specialist (CAS) and Life Coach who specializes in the Autism and Special Needs Population. She works with adults on the spectrum, parents of autistic children and adults, spouses of adults on the spectrum, and anyone affected by autism or other related special needs. Visit her website to learn more:
www.asnlifecoach.com
asnlifecoach@gmail.com
Twitter: @asnlifecoach
Facebook: https://www.facebook.com/AutismAndSpecialNeedsLifeCoach

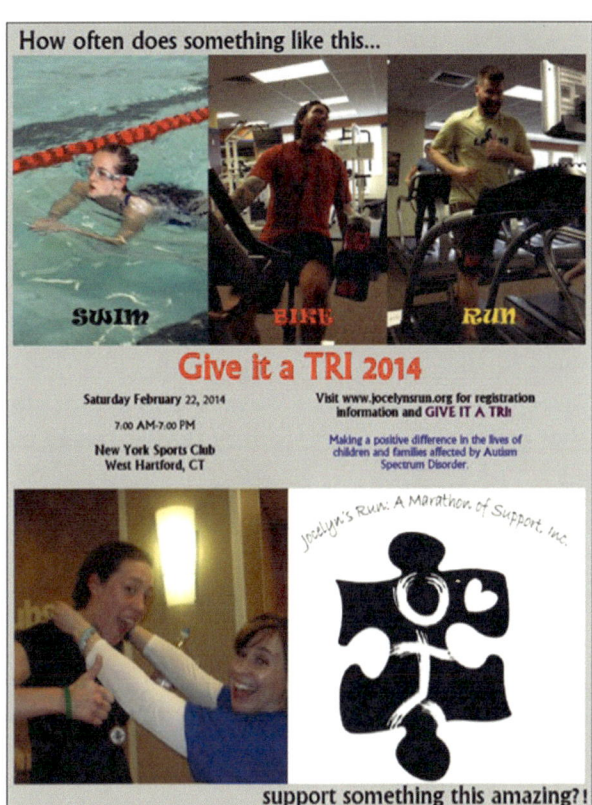

AUTISM COACH NUTRITIONAL SUPPORT

Helping individuals within the autism spectrum reach their maximum potential since 2000.

Supplements
- Carefully chosen, high quality
- Full potency, bioactive
- Gluten/casein free
- Free of common allergens
- Cutting edge/research based
- Support many protocols
- Autism Coach product line

See reviews of our products on the US Amazon website.

Pantry Staples
- Gluten/casein free
- Non-GMO
- Cooking oils
- Gluten free oats

Have a question? We know our products and can share our thoughts as one member of the autism community to another.

Ethical, family-oriented company started by a parent spectrum with a child on the spectrum. If we won't use a product ourselves, we won't sell it to you.

www.autismcoach.com
Email: contactautismcoach@gmail.com

(Autism Coach ships directly within the US. Autism Coach line products are also available in the UK at yourhealthbasket.co.uk and in Europe at detoxpeople.eu)

SENSORY FUN

Leslie Burby

BINS

I live in New England, which for those of you not familiar with the United States is a group of states that gets to witness what every season has to offer.

We get blizzards, we get heat waves, and we are well known for our beautiful foliage; when the leaves turn such vibrant colors that some give the illusion of being on fire.

So during the winter months when temperatures plummet and we get extremely cold temperatures, I can't exactly get my kids to play outside safely, which is why I try to get creative with playing options. However, I don't like to clean nor do I have the time to clean. These things have led me to my love of bins. That's right – bins! Plastic bins that the children can play with and then I can quickly throw a lid on it and store it on a shelf for another day. My favorite bins are the ones that have a locking or snap top. How much fun can playing in a bin be? What can you possibly put in a bin that would be considered fun sensory play? Glad you asked.

My answer: popcorn seeds (not the buttered kind), uncooked noodles (try different kinds curly rigatoni, smooth like ziti, etc.), dried beans, uncooked rice, corn starch, salt, craft sand or playground sand, baking soda, etc. One of these items in a bin at a time with some small hidden toys can prove to combine sensory stimuli and fun. You might have a bin of popcorn seeds for four days with a list of items that the child needs to look for such as: Barbie's pink shoe, Toy car, paper clip, a stamp, a whistle, a hair bow, a puzzle piece, an individually wrapped candy (Hershey kisses or chocolate gold coins are good options.) For added fun I include sand toys. A shovel and a sand spinner can provide and more ways to play and add an audio component. The sound of popcorn seeds and uncooked is always interesting. For smooth items you can have children dig for items but you can also have them write or draw using their fingers. Let us know what you put in your bins. Post your pictures on our [Facebook page](#) or on our [Pinterest page](#).

SENSORY CLASSROOM TIP

Most children with autism have proprioceptive difficulties, which becomes evident when they are required to write and draw in school.

For some, they press too hard and are constantly breaking crayons and snapping pencil tips. Whereas others do not press hard enough leaving faint marks on the paper that are hard to see. If you have a child that is pressing too hard, try rolling up a paper towel or a small bouncy ball and putting it in their palm, it naturally forces the hand to lessen the grip. For the child that doesn't press down hard enough add weight to their pencil or pen. How? I used washers. For added fun, I paint them with nail polish and then let the kids pick out what colors they want. This also helps lessen the teasing factor from other children who will ask why they have a metal washer on their pencil. If the washer is painted now all of sudden it is a pencil decoration or accessory. The boys don't need to know you used nail polish as your paint medium. Nowadays you can get a variety of colors

SENSORY FUN

or nail polish, not just red and pink. For even sensory fun, buy the scented nail polish. I like the Revlon scented nail polish. They have scents such as bubble gum, and icy grape. Scents have been found to increase attention. To make sure the washers don't slide off use an elastic band on each end.

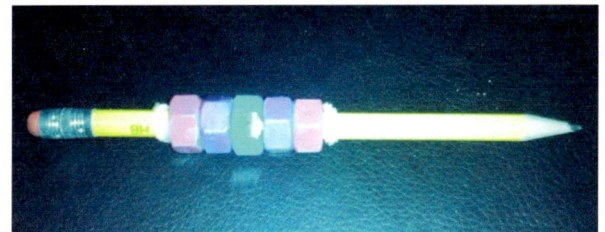

YOUR DAY, YOUR WAY: THE AUTISM/ SPECIAL NEEDS DAILY ORGANIZER APP

By Brooke Twine

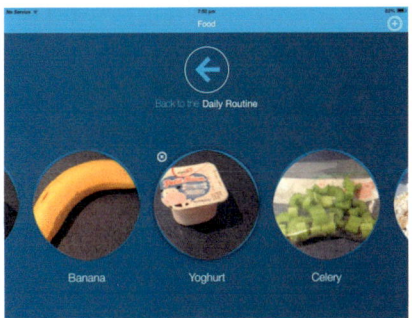

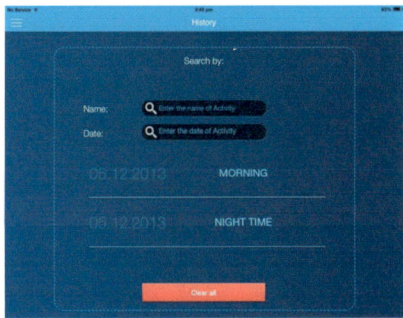

https://www.youtube.com/watch?v=prv0GNcNwdI#t=4

At 2 and 4 months my little boy was given a provisional diagnosis of Autism and at 3, the diagnosis was officially confirmed. It was at this time the onslaught of professionals began. We had a GP, a pediatrician, a child psychologist, a speech therapist and an occupational therapist. Mummy and son were quickly becoming overwhelmed.

As any parent would, I was determined to do the best for my son but I was exhausting and frustrating him and the family in the process. The most frustrating moments for him were during those times when the therapists and I were using daily routines and request boards with him. I had multiple pieces of cardboard with pictures of activities or food printed onto them. I would show them to my son to encourage him to request items that he wanted or to follow a routine for an activity. He would just glance at the board and very smoothly attempt to saunter away. I was persistent and would follow him. The smooth saunter would pick up the pace and become a steady jog, then a run. I maintained my encouraging voice hoping and hoping that we would respond. He did respond and as he

SENSORY FUN

> **"The app allows me to create a profile for my son and program an entire day, week or month, complete with written and visual instructions that run in real time, using all of my own photographs."**

is non-verbal, he responded in the most determined way he could. He turned, grabbed the cardboard and launched an attack. He ripped some of it, folded the rest in half and ran and hid it! There had to be an easier way.

One night in 2012 before heading off to sleep, I pondered what I could do to help him to request items and prepare for his day. I had about 5 different apps on my iPad but they were not engaging him. I thought to myself, "I wish I had an app that did routines, activities and requests all in one." It was time to get proactive and get it developed myself.

I sourced a number of options but found myself pulling back and second-guessing the process. This year I decided I needed to act. I knew this was going to be useful for my son, so perhaps it would be of benefit to others too. My husband and I decided to fund the project ourselves so we contacted the developers at Edway App Studio and moved into a very exciting stage in our lives.

The "Autism/Special Needs Daily Organizer" for iPad is now complete and available on the App Store. I have been using it consistently with my son, he doesn't run, in fact, he laughs at the pictures of himself that appear and intently focuses on the content. The app allows me to create a profile for my son and program an entire day, week or month, complete with written and visual instructions that run in real time, using all of my own photographs. The daily routine can be put on pause if I get behind or I can mark an activity as completed so my son and I can prepare for the next part of our busy day. This is also great for teachers as multiple profiles can be created on the one purchase.

There are pre-set request boards called "Family," "Food," "Play," and "I Want," which are customizable with my own photographs. There is also an "I Feel" board, which has set avatars that communicate happy, sad and angry. I can also create my own custom request boards, which is great for items like toilet training, which is somewhat a tad too unpredictable to put on a daily routine with a specific time! We are also planning some awesome updates that also allow for audio so when my son points to a request, he can also hear the word being said through my recorded voice.

Life with a child with a diagnosed ASD is a life of triumphs, anarchy, joy and frustrations. It is a life that is constantly on the go and full of surprises. The "Autism/Special Needs Daily Organizer" was designed to help my son and I on this journey and it is my sincere hope that it can assist others on their journey too.

To download the "Autism/Special Needs Daily Organizer" from the App Store, please visit: https://itunes.apple.com/au/app/autism-special-needs-daily/id751268885?mt=8

To access a User Guide for the "Autism/Special Needs Daily Organizer" and also my blog please visit my website, Autism – Seriously? at: www.autismseriously.com

Please come and connect with me on Facebook at: https://www.facebook.com/AutismSeriously and on Twitter @AutismSeriously

To learn more about my wonderful app developers please visit: http://www.edwayapps.com.au

---

BIO:

Brooke Twine is a high school teacher in the UK and the mother of a 6 year old boy who was diagnosed with autism in 2009. High school teacher + mother = sliding scale to insanity!! My husband's name is Ashley and he is a coal train driver. My beautiful mother, Debbie, is an integral part of my family who helps us each and every day to raise my son. My little family has been on quite the journey together since the diagnosis, accessing services and endeavoring to find the best combination of professionals to introduce into my son's life. My little boy is non-verbal and not toilet trained, so life can present itself with some challenges. We are determined to maintain our positivity, even in those moments when I could have a meltdown that easily surpasses that of my son.

DAUGHTER'S PERSPECTIVE

How I Wish I knew
MY FATHER HAD ASPERGER'S SYNDROME

Dr. Mary A. Houser

There is no doubt in my mind that my father was on the autism spectrum. At the time when he was born, 1922, autism had not yet been identified as a developmental disability, so he never received an official diagnosis. I would guarantee today, however, based on the diagnostic criteria for autistic disorder that he had Asperger's Syndrome.

What I remember best about Dad was the desperation that I felt as a child not being able to develop a typical father-daughter relationship with him. At a very basic level, I just wanted him to hug me and tell me that he loved me. He didn't. As a younger child, I wanted him to carry photos of me in his wallet and proudly show his friends. He didn't. As a teenager, I wanted him to ask me about the boys I liked. He didn't. He couldn't. He had no understanding of social relationships or how to develop and maintain them. He was a man who lived deep within himself. Concrete walls surrounded him and there were no doors or secret passageways to his inside.

DAUGHTER'S PERSPECTIVE

There was no warmth between Dad and me. There was little connection. I felt ignored. He didn't seem interested in knowing me. Growing up I tried reasoning with myself about this difference and thought perhaps our lack of relationship was attributed to generational issues, him being "old school" and all. During the time when Dad was raised, children were revered as second class citizens and intimate relationships between parents and children were not typically formed. Perhaps this is why he behaved that way towards me, I contemplated. That was until later in my life when I examined his relationships with other adults and determined that they were no different than ours. His colleagues, too, described him as distant, odd, and un-engaging.

> ↘ AS A CHILD, I COULD NOT HAVE UNDERSTOOD THE RAMIFICATIONS OF HAVING A FATHER WITH ASPERGER'S OR HOW IT WOULD HAVE AFFECTED ME.

When Dad died at age 78, I felt there was so much left unknown about him. I had spent many of my youthful hours trying to figure out how to have a relationship with him. It just didn't happen. Was it me? Was I a bad child? Didn't I show enough affection towards him? These questions never got answered. Never could I have imagined that my father had a developmental disability. After all, he was an Episcopal priest and more ironically, a pastoral counselor.

Oddly enough, I knew Dad loved me. He was an excellent provider and a respected professional. He always wanted the best for our family. The problem was that as a child, I didn't care about any of that. I just wanted a dad. More than anything, I loved him and knowing what I know today about autism spectrum disorders, I wish that I could have helped him.

As a child, I could not have understood the ramifications of having a father with Asperger's or how it would have affected me. I imagine that if someone had told me about Dad's disability it would have gone in one ear and out the other. Children cannot comprehend the complexity of a disability but they can sense when something is amiss, even in something as intricate as a father-daughter relationship. Children instinctually seek what helps them to develop into healthy adults. First and foremost, this means a quality relationship with their parents, regardless of an existing disability. More specifically, this means feeling loved. Most children do not expect perfection from their parents but they must feel loved in order to develop emotionally. The key to a better father-daughter relationship for me would have been a stronger outward demonstration of my Dad's love. Although I intellectually knew that he loved me, as a child I needed concrete evidence of his affection. So, what exactly does this mean? How could my father have achieved this goal? Each individual with an ASD presents his own unique characteristics and every adult parents his own way. I can only speak on behalf of my own experiences, but I would have benefitted from Dad spending more time with me and showing an interest in my activities as a child. I participated in several activities as a youngster from horseback riding to playing the piano. Taking me to my riding lessons or listening to me practice the piano would have shown me that he desired a more intimate relationship. In reality, this goal can be fairly easily achieved but requires conscientious effort. It is also important for Aspergerian fathers to be sensitive towards their daughter's feelings. While Dad was not insensitive, he was neutral. Dad could have done things such as hold my hand when I was feeling down or wiped my tears when I skinned my knee to outwardly demonstrate his love. These actions may seem simple but have a lasting effect on the father-daughter relationship.

Perhaps the greatest gift fathers with Asperger's Syndrome can give to their daughters is this outward demonstration of love. This might need to be practiced or even learned how to do properly, but I can guarantee you that it's the most valuable bestowal they can give to their daughters. Girls want their fathers' love no matter if there is disability present or not. It is priceless.

Bio:

Dr. Houser is an assistant professor of Special Education at West Chester University (PA). She is a mother, aunt, and daughter to individuals on the autism spectrum. Her research agenda focuses on families of students with autism spectrum disorders and home/school relationships.